—SKY—
TRUCKS
★★USA★★

SKY TRUCKS USA

AUSTIN J BROWN AND MARK R WAGNER

Acknowledgements

For Fiona and Annette
Grateful thanks go to the whole team at Hawkins & Powers: Dan Hawkins & Gene Powers, Charlie Rennelson, Tom Risk, Bob Buc, Mike Lynn, Claude Tyrell, Fawn Goton and Annette Dillon to name but a few; Mark Bickum of the US Forestry Service at Grand Junction; Duane Zantop of Zantop International and Deane Melvin of Trans Continental Airlines at Willow Run; Harry Delno at Sandford; Mark Mispagel at Macavia in Santa Rosa; Ted Vallas of Air Resorts at Carlsbad Palomar; James Kane of Northwest Airlink and John Lynch of Lynch Flying Services at Billings; Jan Reifenberg of Tanker 13; Gene Day and Vernon Thorp of the Kamikaze B-25; Walter Houghton of Broward County Aviation Department; Richard Wheeler of Systems International at Barstow; Randall Brenneman of Trans World Express at Meigs Field, Chicago; and last but not least, our friend Phil Geddes down in Escondito.

All the photographs that appear in this volume were shot using Nikon equipment, loaded with Kodachrome 64 or 200 ASA film.

First published in 1991 by Osprey, a division of Reed Consumer Books Limited, Michelin House, 81 Fulham Road, London SW3 6RB
Reprinted 1998

ISBN 185532 771 6

Editor Tony Holmes
Design Paul Kime
Printed in Hong Kong

For a catalogue of all books published by Osprey Aerospace please write to:

The Marketing Department, Osprey Publishing, 1st Floor, Michelin House, 81 Fulham Road, London SW3 6RB

Title page Looking more like an albatross around someone's neck rather than the valuable low-time Grumman UH-16A that it really is, this specimen should have been up and flying on California's airshow circuit for the 1990 season

Right Sporting slightly fewer blades than an electric razor, Polair's Tri Turbo-3 DC-3 conversion was parked up at Bakersfield contemplating another season at the Pole. The design has just been beaten into second place by a Dash 7 conversion for an aircraft in the intermediate range between the Twin Otter and the C-130 for inclusion in the British Antarctic Survey's fleet for 1991

Introduction

It is now four years since the publication of our first follow-up book on Stephen Piercey's famous sky truck theme, and this has turned out to be our biggest challenge yet. Trying to illustrate the propliner scene across the whole of the continental United States simultaneously, we had a good idea where most of the aircraft were based, but with the active ones, particularly the fire bombers, they proved very evasive as they came under the control of the Forestry Service and moved from fire to fire more or less at will. The number of times I arrived somewhere just to see a blank space where they had been was quite frustrating – they just kept putting the damn fires out and moving on!

Mark carved a line out from northern Florida through the southern states to Los Angeles, digging himself out of snow in Texas in what we assumed would be a mild winter, whilst I worked my way across from Detroit and Chicago to the wide open spaces of Montana and Wyoming, over Colorado and on to San Francisco and LA. During our travels one thing became clear; these old timers are not going to fade away that easily, and there are young pilots around who prefer to fly these things rather than jets because they just love them. And there's no end to a relationship like that. So keep your eyes open for more conversions and rebuilds, and in the meantime, keep this book to hand as a statement in time.

Austin J Brown & Mark R Wagner
London & Bristol, 1991

Right Otis Spunkmeyer's DC-3 N97H offers sentimental journeys out of Oakland, California, over the picturesque San Francisco Bay area. You can find it at the North Terminal by the Short Solent flying boat. It is luxuriously appointed to carry 18 passengers, and a second aircraft is planned to join it soon

Contents

Douglas designs

DC-3D N3759Q of Express Airways Inc faces the widest collection of Twin Beech variants I have yet seen anywhere, including two Pacair Tradewinds, at Sandford, Florida, in 1988

Above Job done, closed up, and ready for departure, N19906 is fit again

Left After cleaning up the magneto on the port engine, this Majestic Airlines DC-3 returned to Salt Lake City from Billings, Montana, where it is a regular visitor

Above EASI line-up. Note the tin cans on the pitot heads to keep the bugs out

Left My back feels like this mule looks after 26 years of flying, so how does this DC-3 feel after 50? One of EASI's sprayers at Belle Glade in central Florida, a misnomer if ever I heard one. With a foul smelling sugar cane processing plant on site, and the place dubbed 'AIDS City', it hasn't got a lot going for it, apart, that is, from the mosquitoes!

Above Pulling out of Tico at the Valiant Air Command Show, this ex-Danish Air Force C-47A retracts its undercarriage in the traditional way (right leg first) as the 50-year-old hydraulics take the strain

Right Detail of the tail spray gear on an anti-Mosquito DC-3 based at Naples in the spring of 1988

Above Take the turnpike turn-off to Tamiami if you fancy buying this C-47 (N46949) for US $120,000, or near offer. The ex-Canadian Air Force machine was operated by Aeroservicos Honduras during the late 1980s hauling food, clothes and who knows what else around Honduras, Guatemala and El Salvador

Right Marathon County Mosquito Control DC-3s stare down the active runway during the low season in the Florida Keys in March 1988

Above This beautiful C-54E (N9013V), parked up at Billings, belongs to Lynch Flying Service, who, in addition to a fleet of modern light aircraft, operate four B-26 Invaders. At the time of my visit one of them was writing off Pratt & Whitney R2800s at a great rate performing accelerate/stops for a film

Right Steaming down the final approach just 100 feet above 'Spanky's Drive Thru' come the 'Gas Guzzlin Gringos of Occupied Mexico'. Based at Laredo in southern Texas, American Air Freight operate two DC-4s. This is N96448, with all four engines working!

Above The American Air Freight logo above the hangar door at Laredo

Left Close behind N96448, N74AF returns to base from Torreon, Mexico, with the number one prop feathered due to a faulty intake manifold which had reduced the manifold pressure to the ambient level. All in a day's work for Chas Taylor's boys in the cockpit. Captain Don Deming flew many an interesting mission in Laos during the Vietnam War, followed by a stint flying a Gulfstream 2 based in Borneo, before returning to the world of piston power at Laredo. First Officer Biff Bellon used to fly DC-7s with the Arizona-based forest firefighters, T & G Aviation

Above Back on the ground, both aircraft get a thorough once over, which includes engine runs. A DC-4 averages between 10 and 12 hours of maintenance per flying hour and carries about 20,000 lbs of cargo. This compares with 13–15 hours for a DC-6 which carries 30,000 lbs, and 8–9 hours for the Curtiss C-46 with a payload of 12,000 lbs. During the 1970s and early 1980s the northern back of the Rio Grande was rife with contraband flyers who would land on 'unlicensed' airstrips. The sudden decline in this type of operation over the past three years has shocked some pilots. 'Nowadays you take your passport with you, and you have to pay landing fees', explained Captain Don Hopp. 'To get out of Mexico six copies of the flight plan must be signed and stamped in six different offices, and tips given to grease the administrative wheels, followed by more tips for refuellers and customs officers or else they'll go to lunch and hold you up!'

Right and overleaf Travelling along Route 66 through Arizona from the Grand Canyon one stumbles upon Kingman, a mass of alluring neon motel signs all advertising $16 queen-bedded rooms with telephones. The town's airport, adjacent to the Santa Fe Express railroad, was once home to many Boeing 707s in desert storage. More recently, three immaculate DC-4s owned by Aeroflite have moved in. N96358 is kitted out as a water bomber to carry a 2000-gallon load and wears the tail number 160, whilst N811E is a sprayer and N91802 is a freighter. The only other non-GA resident in the Spring of 1989 was the rear half of one of American Trans Air's 707s, wearing the serial N7515A. By the way, if you're interested in chartering a DC-4 call the airport and ask to speak to Matt or Jim

Right An impressive desert sunset engulfs a DC-4 at Kingman

Right Long-term resident of Fort Lauderdale's Jet Aviation ramp, DC-6 N906MA looks like it may at last be going places. The same cannot, however, be said for the Dow Jones Company's rapidly disappearing Convairliner

Below Taking a break from spraying, Biegert Aviation's DC-4s remain in storage until needed. The company has a history dating back to 1949, and over the years targets have included spruce bud worms in Maine between 1976 and 1980, mosquitos in Florida, Mediterranean fruit fly on the Mexico-Guatemala border in 1979, and thousands of hours of bud worm work in Canada before Conifair took over. Based at Chandler Memorial Airfield in the Gila River Indian Reservation, Arizona, Biegert Aviation has more recently diversified into the property and insurance business to complement its spraying activities. Scattered around in the background of this photograph are the silhouettes of T & G's DC-7 fleet

Overleaf The patched bullet holes on the port side of N1037F's nose, just below the windshield, may cause one to wonder what this old 'contraband crock' has been up to since it appeared in *Big Props* when it was with Seagreen in Antigua. Could it be true that the DC-6 was shot at in mid air by the US DEA (Drug Enforcement Agency) whilst re-entering US airspace at night with no lights on? Well maybe, but more likely is the story that it was shot at on the ground in Mexico whilst performing a somewhat unorthodox transaction at a remote landing strip. The one fact which all the gossip mongers do agree upon was that the aircraft commander was killed in the incident, and the co-pilot continued the flight back into the USA. American Air Freight later acquired the 'old Doug' during the summer of 1988 from Central Air Service (CAS) of Tucson, Arizona, in a part exchange deal for C-47 XB-DYU. CAS acquired the aircraft from Davis-Monthan air force base after it had been impounded by the US authorities

Firebombers

Left A working 'four, and a very hard working 'four at that! ARDCO's Tanker 152 N9015Q lifts off the runway at Grand Junction in Colorado to make yet another drop of retardant on a nearby forest fire

Below A low sun emphasizes the size of the tank mod on the belly of this DC-4 as it climbs out with all four R-2000s straining at max take-off weight

Above It's good to take a shower at the end of a long, hot, dusty day, particularly when it's given by a young lady!

Left And Marilyn Monroe flies on every trip! Third window from the rear, port side, is a cardboard cutout of our best known blonde. Tanker 152 taxies in for another top up of Fire-trol, whereas I'm sure Marilyn would have just settled for a large gin and tonic

Above Nose to nose, these two DC-6Bs eyeball each other at Macavia's Santa Rosa base in northern California. Macavia has recently modified the first BAe 748 for tanker duties through the Cranfield Institute of Technology in England, operating it in France during the 1990 season

Left On its return, the DC-4's aft fuselage bears the scars of the last drop, the airflow etched into the liquid concentrate in fluid flow lines

Above N96451 is one of ten waterbombing DC-4s operated by Central Air Service around California and Kansas. The company, owned by Bill Dempsay, is based at Tucson, where CAS undertake refits, maintenance and storage of all types of piston-engined aircraft

Left Working out of Grand Junction on the same fire as the DC-4 was this P2V-7 Neptune up from Almagordo in New Mexico. Although it is based there, the Neptune will probably never see Almagordo during the season because, as C-54 skipper Jan Reifenberg's visiting card says, 'Home is where the prop stops!'

Above Tanked up for another trip, N4235T is marshalled off the blood red ramp, stained with Fire-trol spilled during the last top up. The red and white flash on the fuselage gives a clue to its Royal Canadian Air Force ancestry

Left Head-on view of the Black Hill's Neptune, taxying back in from a drop; you can see the extent of the tank mod on the underbelly. When the first tanker mods were made, the only requirement was for the load to be dropped fairly crudely onto the fire as one mass of retardant, and for the centre of gravity of the aircraft to remain within the flight envelope throughout the operation. They found, however, that one giant mass of extinguishant could have the opposite effect, especially if it landed directly on the fire; it would just blow the fire out in all directions. So they then arranged for the retardant to be released through a number of hopper doors running fore and aft along the fuselage, producing a stream which could be laid in lines around the edge of the fire

Above A jetless Neptune at Stockton being refuelled for the next sortie. Aero Union have completely reworked these aircraft, removing the jets and associated systems, thereby lightening them considerably. Their conversion is also more aerodynamic than the others as there is no external tank, the Fire-trol being carried internally with release doors flush to the underbelly

Left With the help of its two Westinghouse J34 turbojets, 35 Tango sings its way into the air against the background of the Book Cliffs at Grand Junction. The jets are used for take-off as auxiliary powerplants, and then switched off to be relit again to provide boost during the drop and overshoot. They would appear to be an indispensable asset at first glance, but I was told that the fuel tankage and associated plumbing weighs so much that they almost cancel each other out—hence the decision by Aero Union to take them off their Neptunes

Right Tanker 03 framed by one of the Aero Union's Cessna O2A Super Skymasters, which act as forward air controllers over the fire. Firefighters and equipment are also parachuted into the blaze to try to control the fire, and the O2A can be very useful as a guardian angel in the event of them getting trapped by the flames

Below Hawkins & Powers A-26 Invader taxies in after a flight test at its base at Greybull

Above The Invader parked up on the ramp. The venerable bomber will soon be phased out of service as a fleet of Lockheed C-130A Hercules have just been bought at auction for conversion to the tanker role. The C-119 in the background no longer flies on active service as too many were lost during the previous season and their certification was withdrawn. The immaculate company Beech E-18S completes the picture

Right The aeriel view of Hawkins & Powers' base at Greybull shows how the airfield sits on a plateau above the town. The Wyoming scenery is as amazing as the number of propliners on the ramp

Above Known affectionately in the military as the 'C Dash Crash', the C-119 Flying Boxcar was a great workhorse in the firefighting business, but had its certification withdrawn at the end of the 1988 season following several fatal losses in operation. It was alleged that the wings came off in the drop through the airframe being overstressed, the accidents being unsurvivable as the C-119s were operating over a raging inferno when they occurred

Right Close-up of C-119G N39351 Tanker 139 (also an ex-RCAF machine), shows the mounting of its J34 auxiliary turbojet on top of the fuselage, complementing its two Wright Cyclone R-3350s

EMPTY WT - 42,120
GROSS WT - 72,500
LANDING WT - 69,970
CONTRACT LOAD - 18,000
NORMAL OP WT - 66,410

Above Smokey Rides Again! Smokey Bear, the ad man's warrior against starting forest fires, rides astride a Privateer cartoon on the side of this C-119

Right Two of Hemet Valley Aviation's C-119s put out to grass at their southern California base. C-130As are destined to take over their work, too

Above Owned by DMI Aviation, which has its own massive compound bordering onto the desert storage facility at Davis-Monthan AFB, this C-119 is one of two Flying Boxcars in overspill storage on the CAS ramp at Tucson International Airport

Right One of Hemet's bug-eyed S-2A Trackers (N442DF) sitting on the pan at Chico

Above This US-2B, N5243A, sits quietly in the grass at Stockton until its time comes to be converted. Perhaps it will get a completely new lease of life as a Marsh Turbo S-2, replacing its two Wright R-1820 piston engines with 1250 shp Garrett TPE-331 turbines

Right What a gem! I chased this PB4Y-2 Privateer from Greybull in Wyoming to Grand Junction in Colorado, just missing it by minutes en route at Denver. Built for the US Navy in 1945, the PB4Y-2 was the Navy's modified version of the Liberator. Old it may be, but low on hours and immaculate it is too. And it does the job well. Seen here just rotating the No 1 engine prior to start, it worked a fire alongside the Black Hills Neptune and the ARDCO C-54, quelling it within a day

Above This shot of Tanker 121 emphasizes the sheer size of its single fin, which replaced the Liberator's twin fins under the Navy requirement. And you could grow palms in the glasshouse in the nose!

Left The Privateer climbs out against the backdrop of Mount Garfield on its never ending rotation of sorties during the day

Above In contrast to the previous two Privateers, this one is permanently grounded in the Yankee Air Force Museum at Willow Run Airport, just outside of Detroit, at Ypsilanti. Having force-landed near Vancouver, it was shipped here and will be restored as N6813D

Left Privateer 123 positioned over to Grand Junction when another forest fire broke out in the region. Like its more stylishly painted sister ship, it too was built in 1945, one of a total of 740 for the US Navy, and is likewise a low-hour airframe

Convair and Curtiss

Left Convair county USA. C-131s at the Aircraft Maintenance and Regeneration Center (AMARC), Davis-Monthan AFB

Below Hamilton Aviation at Tucson International undertake all sorts of major aircraft refitting. Here Convair 580 N94215 (retired from service with American Airlines in 1988) undergoes a complete overhaul and the installation of a side cargo door before delivery to DHL's European hub at Brussels

Yet more Convairliners. Literally hundreds of Convair medium twins were used by the armed forces throughout the 1950s, 60s and into the 70s. Besides performing as the workhorse for Military Airlift Command, C-131s flew as navigation trainers (T-29s), VIP transports (VC-131s) and naval freighters (R4Ys). Now they all rest side by side under the sweltering Arizona sun

Above A one-time 'old chestnut' of Fort Lauderdale, Convair 440-40 N411GA (featured in *Miami Props*) changed hands for US $165,000 during the late 1980s. Anticipating passenger routes to Monterrey and San Antonio, 'GA had been refitted, modified and issued with a new FAA part 135 certificate. Sporting the new Laredo Air livery, the 'good as new' Convairliner awaits its time for action

Above left Proudly labelled as Laredo's international flight by airport director Jose Luis Flores, Convair 580 N32KA of Laredo Air makes three or four passenger flights a day to Monterrey in north east Mexico. This aircraft was previously owned by Resorts International of California, and joined the Laredo operator when the service started early in 1988

Below left Convair 440-40 Metropolitan N136CA going through a detailed four-week long overhaul in preparation for active service with Laredo Air. Manufactured in 1957 and previously registered N37444, this airframe was the 400th aircraft manufactured

Left The Central Air Service ramp at Tucson International sends you back in time with its booming rock hits of the 1950s and 60s played by 'KOLD Tucson' and listened to by engineers, in addition to the wealth of propliners present. The Braniff Convair 340, owned by Clarke Cryderman and still wearing its original colour scheme, is in for a cargo door refit to accommodate igloo-type containers, and was due to fly by 1990. According to a report in *Propliner* magazine by Charles R Stewart, this aircraft served with Braniff until 1967, when it suffered an engine fire. Before its retirement it had flown a total of 31,000 hours in 14 years, it and other '340s being replaced in the Braniff ranks by Lockheed Electras and Boeing 707s. The airline gave the Convairliner to John R Morey, who started repairing the engine, before finally putting the aircraft into storage at Barstow Airport, California. There it stayed for over 20 years, its windows being smashed, cockpit instruments stolen, and several bullet holes appearing in the tail from passing vandals. Cryderman, president of Century Airlines (a DC-3 and CV-440 operator based at Pontiac, Michigan), bought the '340 in November 1988 and made it airworthy once again

Below Petal cowlings on the Convairliner series make the engines much more accessible for maintenance. Photographed at Fort Lauderdale in April 1988, this CV-440 Metropolitan (N411GA) of Sunbird Air had encountered engine problems and was temporarily grounded

Above Showing a certain amount of character in its face wearing the wraparound Trans Continental colour scheme, this Metropolitan shares Willow Run with two sister-ships, all modified to Convair 440 standard, along with four DC-6s and eight DC-8s

Left Curtiss C-46F-1-CU N777AF of July 1945-vintage, is seen here at Laredo in January 1989 during an FAA check. The Commando, which flew as '857' in the Bay of Pigs operation in September 1961, had not flown for some months but was deemed airworthy, having no major snags. The 'torching' effect from the red hot engine exhausts is quite normal for large piston powerplants when a high power setting is applied. One of the regular captains to fly 'alpha fox' is Carl Shipman, an ex-Air America C-46 flyer in Laos and Vietnam. After the end of the war in South East Asia, he eventually found his way to the Mexican border where there was always good money available for aircrew prepared to risk being caught by the authorities running contraband goods. The freight often consisted of household electrical items, upon which Mexico used to levy a heavy import tax. A pilot was expected to fly low at night with only his cockpit lights switched on in an effort to avoid detection. Often a beach or remote forest clearing would be used as a runway and the cargo was exchanged strictly for cash. These meetings were often intercepted by Mexican police who had been tipped off, and nearly all the crews who undertook such missions ended up serving time in one of Mexico's 'universities'. Carl himself had a lucky escape following a crash south of the border some years ago. He survived the incident with a smashed face, and several broken bones, in addition to an almost certain two-year prison sentence. However, a Mexican doctor advised that if he went to jail he would probably not survive the ordeal on health grounds, so Carl's case was dropped and he was released

Above Doug Taylor's C-46F (N1663M) previously operated in Alaska in an all-blue scheme, the airframe being stripped back to bare metal in 1989. Built in August 1945, the aircraft has carried the same registration since leaving USAF service. Ordered in March 1944 as one in a batch of 234 'F models, the C-46 cost US $233,377 to construct. The aircraft was reported to have skidded off the end of the runway at Arctic Village, Alaska, on 22 January 1975 during a supposed take-off roll. There were no fatalities and the aircraft was swiftly repaired

Right Although based at McAllen, Texas, for normal operations, N1663M flew to Laredo for some attention to its number one engine. The 'F variant of the C-46 is powered by two R-2800-75s each producing 2000 hp, and is basically a C-46A wearing Hamilton props and without control boost, producing a top speed of 220 kts

Oddities

Scenic Airlines of Las Vegas still occasionally fly this 1929-vintage Ford 5ATC Trimotor on special charters, usually around the Grand Canyon during the summer months. Insured for US $1.6 million, N414H, with 10 passenger seats plus two air crew, is powered by three Pratt & Whitney R-985 engines, giving a maximum take-off weight of 4.5 tonnes

Above This C-133B (N2276V) is one of five remaining examples owned by Maurice Carlson. This one is at Tucson International, whilst a pair reside at Mojave, California, and two more in Alaska. Sadly, the Cargomasters are grounded by FAA regulations, but they could find their way into museums or perform other static uses. How about an indoor golf course or football pitch?

Right Behind the Las Vegas Tropicana, this C-124C Globemaster is destined to become a restaurant and night club. To label this a long term project would be no underestimation, so in the meantime you may like to try the Tropicana's blackjack table or *folies bergeres* show. The hulk was flown to 'Vegas from Davis-Monthan AFB following a period of storage. Currently registered N3153F, it previously saw military service with the Georgia Air National Guard as 53-0044

What do you get when you cross a traction engine, a greenhouse and a quadruple thickness skipping rope? Well, the cockpit of a once-trans-Atlantic airliner may not be the response on the tip of your tongue but . . . Boeing C-97, XA-PII, pilots' eye view, CAS ramp Tucson

Above Less than ten Douglas Cargomasters exist today of the fifty which were delivered to the USAF Military Air Transport Service in the late 1950s. At that time the type could carry double the payload of its predecessors. Continuing the theme of enormity, the C-133B cockpit is more like a small apartment. In addition to the workstations for captain, co-pilot and navigator, there are two large bunk beds, and enough room between all that lot to do the fandango!

Right A couple of yards back from the pilot's quarters on the starboard side in the C-97 cockpit is the flight engineer's panel. Only the 'asymmetric anti-icing twin-tub turbo-boosted Budweiser dispenser pre-stall warning lights' seem to have been omitted on this particular model

Above N145RA is a Vickers Viscount operated by Viscount Air Services of Tucson. Kitted out with 20 seats in a two × two configuration in the rear cabin, and seven luxury seats in the forward compartment, this lively example of the world's favourite British airliner had just finished transporting rock star Rod Stewart, plus entourage, on his concert tour of mainland USA

Right Amongst the orderly chaos of the Hill ramp at Fort Lauderdale, Douglas C-47 N700RG was for sale in the spring of 1988, following the demise of its would-be operator, Key West Airways

Above All change! Aeropacifico's KC-97 XA-PII gets a replacement powerplant at Tucson

Left What a shock I had when I was thrown out of the tunnel in this B-25 to find myself in the glass nose hurtling down towards the runway at Tico in a simulated airfield attack! I'd taken off strapped in behind the crew, and was then given permission to transfer into the bomb aimer's nose position once airborne. As I slid into the tunnel head-first, the aircraft went into a dive, and I was ejected headlong into the field of view. This photo tells it all. Thinking that the worst was over, I crawled back into the tunnel for landing, only to find myself lying on the floor behind the crew, which I then realised by the gaps in it, was really the aircraft's bomb doors. Sweaty moment number two!

Above XA-PII was operated by Transportes de Carga Aeropacifico SA de CV
on a daily hop carrying fresh bread between Bimbo Bread's bakery at La Paz
on the long peninsula of Baja, California, and mainland Mexico. In USAF
service, the KC-97 wore the serial number 53-3816 and left the Aerospace
Maintenance and Regeneration Centre (AMARC) at Davis-Monthan AFB in
November 1987

Right The double-decker 'Bimbo Boeing' had experienced a loss of manifold
pressure, and metal shavings were found in the oil of the filter of the massive
28-cylinder Pratt & Whitney R-4300 engine. Supervised by Jack of Central Air
Services, and with the use of a crane, the entire job was completed in a day.
When the word hit the ramp that in Mexico the same feat takes eight days, the
engineers decided to seek employment south of the border and spend six days a
week on the beach

Above On a quiet country road in the heart of Oregon is the 'Flight 97 Restaurant', the 'premises' being another former resident of AMARC

Left The complex eyes of this double-bubbled fuselage KC-97 Stratotanker gaze down on me at the Milestones of Flight Museum in Antelope Valley, California. Now well into its retirement, 53-0272 last flew with the California Air National Guard in the mid 1970s

Above This KC-97 was lot number 25 when it was sold from AMARC, and it is seen here in the spring of 1989 being readied to leave the 20-acre DMI Aviation compound on the edge of Davis-Monthan AFB. A KC-97 with a rear cargo door sells for around US $300,000, and DMI holds enough spares to keep the world's C-97 fleet in the air for another 20 years

Right After a three-hour turnaround at Los Angeles International (LAX), the Southern Air Transport (SAT) Hercules taxies to the 25L holding point. Powered by four Allison 501-D22A turboprops, this aircraft started life in 1970 as an L 100–20, and was later converted to L 382G specs with a maximum take-off weight of over 70 metric tonnes

Above SAT Lockheed L 382G N910SJ cruises down the glide slope for an early morning arrival on runway 25L at LAX

Right This drone-carrying Hercules (hence the designation DC-130A) was photographed at the Mojave flight test facility in July 1989. Though wearing US Navy titles, it carries the US Air Force serial 560514

Above On short finals to land on Nine left at Miami International, Lockheed Electra N358Q, owned by TPI Aviation, trucks in from one of the Dutch Caribbean Islands whilst on lease to ALM in March 1989

Left Perfectly preserved and securely sealed at the DMI pound, this C-130 should be released to bidders with around US$5 million in their pocket. With the recent introduction of the type in the firefighting role, ex-military Hercules should still have a long career ahead of them. The white compound liberally applied to the fuselage is known as Spraylat, the plastic-like sealant being used to protect the airframe from sand, dust and animals. Covering the windshield keeps the cabin temperature down and all internal pipes are generally coated in oil to prevent corrosion before being sealed

Right The STAF Electra, F-OGST, is another regular at Miami International

Above This preserved Boeing B-17 is a fitting memorial to the American Veterans of World War 2, Korea and Vietnam, and is permanently parked by the roadside at Tulare in southern California

Right When cruisin' route 205 through Oregon who could resist buying their gasoline here? And with Lacey's Bomber Inn on the same site selling Shrimp Louis at $4.95, or all you can eat BBQ ribs also at $4.95, including tax, you might as well fill up the family and the car at the same time. According to locals, this B-17G, (44-85790) was 'flown in' around 1970 by owner Art Lacey, who used to allow admirers to climb up inside the Fortress

A goodly screech of rubber on tarmac announced the arrival of DHC-4 N900NC on Tucson International's shorter cross runway, completing its regular Friday evening positioning flight from its Phoenix Skyharbour base. Before closing down the engines one crew member climbed out from the cockpit escape hatch and walked along the port wing to visually check the number two engine. The Caribou is popular with the freight loaders at Tucson's Executive Terminal as, in comparison with the C-47, it is not an up hill struggle to pack the cargo hold

Above N5465, a very smartly painted Fairchild C-123 Provider, stood amongst Costa Rican Caribous at Van Nuys in July 1989

Left For just $100 a month you too could park your classic Connie at Tucson's Ryan Field

Above A panoramic view of the Spruce Goose in its bubble next to the *Queen Mary* at Long Beach, California. Built by Howard Hughes' Hughes Corporation, it made its celebrated flight on Sunday, 2nd November 1946 at low-level for a distance of one mile, and then never flew again

Right The Spruce Goose was nicknamed by members of the press who considered the whole project a joke. Hughes designated it the H-4 Hercules, and powered it with eight 3000 hp Wasp Majors

Above Rick and Randy Grant look after the Short Solent flying boat at Oakland as 'their baby', flanking the aircraft with an incredibly comprehensive museum. They assure me that it will fly again

Right A model of Hughes himself, complete with fedora, sits in the left-hand seat, lending scale to the enormous flight deck which houses state-of-the-art 1940s technology. Looking at it purely as a static exhibit, you have to constantly remind yourself that it did actually fly. Hughes was apparently inspired to built the beast by Henry Kaiser, the shipping magnate, in 1942 when he suggested that the US should build 5000 gigantic flying boats so that it could send troops and arms to the war in 'ships' that could not be torpedoed

Scrap metal

Many aviation scrapyards surround AMARC at Davis-Monthan. This line of work can be risky business as, although being quite sound financially, the storage facilities lie directly below the flightpath of the airbase's A-10 Warthogs. Known to have occasionally dropped canopies and practice bombs, the tank-busters have, according to one yard manager, set his site alight with stray ordnance!

'Cannibalization cul-de-sac', and there's no way out. The damage to this DHC-4 had probably rendered it beyond the point of economical repair at the Western International Aviation site just outside of Tucson

Overleaf Bob's Air Park need not be the last stop for these land locked HU-16s, although their career with the USCG is certainly over

Below A once lively US Navy HU-16 Albatross appears to have been robbed of most saleable items. It is said that a Texas millionaire recently bought and refurbished an ex-San Francisco-based US Coast Guard Albatross for $225,000

Above This Constellation (44-062) flies out of Santo Domingo for a Dominican Republic-based cargo operator. Seen here at DMI Aviation in February 1989, AMSA had already inspected the Connie. A deposit would prompt the fitting of new engines and lifting the aircraft for a gear-swing test, before payment in full ensured delivery

Above left Surrealism is one of the strongest themes experienced around the largest aircraft graveyard in the world. Some scenes may amaze or thrill you, others are a sad end to an aviation era. However, the DMI compound next to AMARC sees many re-vitalized hulks pass through before continuing their flying careers in 'civvie street'. In addition, the compound provides bizarre landscapes for passing photographers. KC-97 bits are DMI's speciality

Below left Well, will it fly or won't it? Probably not, one feels, but it's amazing what you can do with a lot of money

Above Three-bladers, four-bladers and more spinner shapes than you ever dreamt of. If you can't find a prop for your sky truck here you may as well give up

Left Thoroughly robbed of useful parts by the 'save a Connie' team from Kansas, the aircraft's slender lines were due to be reduced to scrap metal within 48 hours of this photo being taken in Tucson in February 1989

Above And the same goes for undercarriage parts too. No less than seven C-97 Stratotankers waiting to continue their lives in the air adorn the background. If you want one call Don Howell at DMI Aviation, Tucson, for a test drive

Above right Two 'sixes and a 'ninety seven at DMI

Below right Like a trussed Christmas turkey, the inverted centre section of a Beech 18 lies in front of a line-up of redundant Provincetown-Boston Martin 404s at Naples, Florida, in 1988. The 404s had to be removed to a remote part of the airfield when illegal immigrants were found to be squatting in them in their previously more accessible parking position. This tends to ruin their second-hand value!

Above Nothing here is necessarily beyond economic repair. C-117s and Albatross at DMI

Above left All the C-47s which enter the DMI pound leave as spare parts or scrap, helping to keep the world's active population of the type in the air

Below left Sold as seen. 'Lovely C-117, one nice lady owner, low mileage, always garaged, never raced or rallied, easy finance terms available, no time wasters please. PS May need new tyres'

The charred remains of C-47 XB-DYP are scattered in a quiet corner of the airfield at Laredo. It is rumoured that the aircraft was heading south of the border with a large haul of contraband electronic goods. The Dakota made a normal take-off roll but on rotation the load is suspected to have shifted back, taking the centre of gravity behind its rear limit for safe flight. The aircraft stalled less than 50 feet above the runway and 'crashed and burned'. Luckily both crew members escaped the wreckage alive but not without a mixture of third degree burns and broken bones

Above Showing definite signs of having rubbed its nose along a runway at some time, this DC-3 was spotted looking the worse for wear in a corner of the ramp at Leigh High Acres, Florida, in 1988

Right The T-29, C-54 and C-118 are commercially sound air freighters in today's economic environment. A good C-54 can sell for around US $175,000, and a C-118 for between US $250 and 500,000, depending on its equipment level and engine age

O-42811

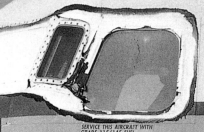

SERVICE THIS AIRCRAFT WITH
GRADE 115/145 FUEL
REFERENCE T. O. 42B1-1-14
U. S. AIR FORCE 5 3-3 2 4 5
A. F. SERIAL NO.
CREW WEIGHT 1200 LBS.

U.S. AIR

STATIC PORT
KEEP HOSE & SURFACE CLEAN
DO NOT PLUG OR BURNISH HOLES

CG041 DPDO

Above This DC-4 used to be operated by Millardair of Canada. Still sporting the old Douglas logo of the 1950s, the sky truck was seen in the National Aircraft compound next to Davis-Monthan AFB in February 1989

Left Tracking days over, these redundant S 2Bs act as a spares source for the Hemet Valley fleet

Above This Douglas A-20 Havoc, which has at some time in its life been converted into an executive aircraft, stands with its wings separated at the Milestones of Flight Museum in Antelope Valley in southern California

Right Cross-eyed and legless, this T-29 resides at the National Aircraft scrapyard

Above Suspended animation. N480RC-F seen through the maze of engines and prop blades of N776M. The Viscount fleet numbers 19 aircraft, three of which are presently operational whilst another seven or eight could be readied for action at short notice. As for the others, well they're just taking it easy, and why not?

Left Desert Dart. Britain's aeronautical bestseller is well represented in the Viscount Air Services corner at Tucson International Airport. Here the prop of N14ORA frames V.748 N24V, which started life as EI-AJV with Aer Lingus. Later it was re-registered G-APNG and operated by BEA and Kuwait Airways, before delivery to the USA. N14ORA is a V.765 and was delivered to the Standard Oil Company in executive configuration in February 1957. During the early 1980s it was leased to Atlantic Gulf Airlines of Florida to serve on their short-lived St Petersburg-Miami scheduled route

Not always just hangin' around, the Viscounts have been regularly chartered by rock bands since the early 1970s for complete tours of the USA. Lured not only by the classic appeal of the aircraft but also by its four-engined safety, large windows, roomy cabins and flexible range of cabin layouts, customers keep on coming back to hire Viscount's machines. Another added bonus is the fact that in over 15 years of operations there have only ever been three maintenance delays. Clients have included Elvis, The Who, Yes, Deep Purple and Led Zeppelin during the 1970s. More recently, Roberta Flack, Chicago, Sting, Stevie Nicks and Jimmy Page have used N15ORC. In the late 1980s, N200RC was chartered by U2, Barry Manilow and Billy Joel, whilst Tina Turner had N24ORC for a while and N145RA still has Rod Stewart's name emblazoned across its nose in dayglo orange

Above Wearing the emblem of Ray Charles Enterprises, this Viscount 800 is not one of those which could be prepared for service at short notice!

Right A prop splits the setting sun at Greybull. Seen from the underwing of a Douglas C-118 sprayer, the Hawkins & Powers' fleet rests in the fading light